Test your knowledge MCQS in Accounting

MAHADEO KESHAV KELKAR

SYLLABUS

SEM III

1	Partnership Final Accounts
2	Piecemeal Distribution
3	Amalgamation of Firms
4	Conversion/Sale of partnership firm into Limited company

SEM IV

1	Introduction to Company Accounts
2	Redemption of Preference shares
3	Redemption of Debentures
4	Profit Prior to Incorporation

Contents:-

Objective questions with model answers on the above topics

1) True or False

2) Match the following

3) Fill in the blanks

(Objective Questions are asked for 20 Marks in Question No.1)

Topic 1 - Partnership Final account.

❖ State whether the following statement is True or False.

1) The Indian Partnership Act was passed in the Year 1932.	True
2) There are two methods of maintaining capital accounts	True
3) Partners are collectively called as Firm and individually called as Partner.	True
4) Under fixed capital method partner current account is Maintained.	True
5) Under Fluctuating capital method partner current account is Maintained.	False
6) The agreement between the partners of a partnership firm is Called as Partnership deed.	True
7) Under Fluctuating Capital Method balance in capital accounts Always remains unchanged.	False
8) Under Fixed capital Method balance in current account changes Every year.	True
9) Partnership deed must be always in written form.	False
10) It is always desirable that the partnership must be in writing.	True
11) In absence of Partnership deed interest on partner loan is allowed at 6% p.a.	True
12) In Absence of Partnership deed no partner is receivable any Interest on his capital.	True
13) In Absence of Partnership deed Partners shares profits and Losses in equal ratio.	True
14) In absence of any provision in Partnership Deed no interest Should be charge on partner's drawings.	True
15) Under Fixed Capital Method interest on partners' capital is Credited to Partners current account.	True
16) Under Fluctuating Capital Method interest on partners' capital is credited to Partners current account.	False
17) Under Fixed Capital Method salary to partners is credited to Partners' current account.	True
18) Under Fluctuating Capital Method salary to partners is credited to Partners current account.	False

19) Goods taken by partner for personal use are credited to Trading account.	True
20) Carriage inwards are debited to Trading accounts.	True
21) Loss of goods because of fire are credited to Profit & Loss account.	False
22) When goods are distributed by way of free sample they credited to Trading account.	True
23) When goods are distributed by way of free sample they debited to Profit & Loss account as an Advertising expenses.	True
24) Credit balance in the trading accounts indicates Gross profit.	True
25) Debit balance in the trading accounts indicates Gross loss.	True
26) Discount received is credited to Trading account.	False
27) Discount given/allowed to customer is debited to Profit & Loss account.	True
28) Bad debts written off during the year are charged to Profit & Loss account.	True
29) Any Interest or dividend received on investment made is credited to Profit & Loss account.	True
30) Bank overdraft is Long term liability of the firm.	False
31) Any amount received as an advance during the year is written on the liability side of the Balance sheet.	True
32) Patents & Copy right is Long term intangible assets of the firm.	True
33) Insurance claim receivable by the firm is written on the asset side of the balance sheet.	True
34) New Partner can be admitted in a firm on any day of the financial year.	True
35) New Partner must bring capital in cash form only.	False
36) On admission of a new partner sacrifice ratio is calculated.	True
37) When new partner is admitted on very first day of the year he is eligible to share profit/loss for the full year.	True
38) On retirement of the partner Sacrifice ratio is calculated.	False
39) Partner may retire from the firm only at the end of the year.	False
40) On retirement of the partner the amount due to the retiring partner remains unpaid, it is transferred to his loan account.	True

41) In case of death of the partner amount payable to the deceased partner is paid to this nominee.	True
42) If in case of death of the partner amount payable to the deceased partner is remain unpaid, it is transferred to his nominee loan account.	True
43) It is said that partner's death is compulsory retirement from the partnership business.	True
44) Liability of partner of a firm is unlimited liability.	True
45) On death of the partner goodwill is not paid to his legal heir.	False
46) Partner of the firm has to conduct lawful business.	True
47) The liability of partner is unlimited.	True

❖ **Match the following:-**

Group A	Group B
1) Sacrifice ratio	a) Intangible asset
2) Gain ratio	b) Agreement between partners
3) The Indian Partnership Act	c) 1932
4) Partnership deed	d) Death of partner
5) Goodwill	e) Admission of partner
6) Live stock	f) Current asset
7) Prepaid expenses	g) Tangible fixed asset

(1- e, 2 - d, 3 - c, 4 - b, 5 - a, 6 - g, 7 - f)

Group A	Group B
1) Profit & Loss A/C	h) Amount irrecoverable from debtors
2) Profit & Loss appropriation A/C	i) Long term liability
3) Trading A/C	j) Staff salary
4) Balance sheet	k) Partners salary
5) Current liability	l) Direct Wages
6) Bank Loan	m) Capital accounts
7) Bad debts	n) Short term liability

(1 – j , 2 – k, 3 – l, 4 –m, 5 – n , 6 –i, 7- h)

Group A	Group B
1) Profit & Loss A/C	o) Shows financial position
2) Drawings by partner	p) Current liability
3) Trading A/C	q) Current Assets
4) Balance sheet	r) In written form or Oral form
5) Bills payable	s) Shows net profit or Loss
6) Closing stock	t) Shows gross profit or Loss
7) Partnership deed	u) Deducted from capital

(1 – s , 2 – u, 3 – t, 4 – o, 5 – p, 6 – q, 7 – r)

❖ Fill in the blank with correct word....

1) The partnership act was passed in the year _______.

2) There are ______ methods of maintaining capital accounts of partners.

3) Cash brought in by the partner is ______ to his capital account.

4) Drawings are _____ to partners' capital account.

5) Capital can be brought in by partner in form of cash and ______ as well.

6) In fixed capital method _____ account is maintained to record the entries like salary, commission to partners.

7) Under ______ capital method balance in capital account changes year by year.

8) _________ is an agreement between the partners.

9) _________ may be in oral form or written form.

10) Liability of partner in partnership is always ______.

11) Minimum ____ partners are required to form partnership business.

12) In absence of deed interest on loan from partners can be maximum __.

13) In absence of any agreement, partners shares profit and losses in

_____ ratio.

14) Any Salary payable to partner is debited to _____ account.

15) New partner cannot be admitted in the firm without the consent of

____.

16) Carriage inwards are debited to _____ account.

17) Carriage outwards are debited to _____ account.

18) Goods taken up by the partner for personal use is treated as _______.

19) Trading accounts shows ______ result in form of gross profit or loss.

20) Goods lost because of theft or fire are credited to ___account.

21) Discount received is credited to _____ account.

22) Payable rent is shown as _____ in the balance sheet.

23) Prepaid rent is shown as _____ in the balance sheet.

24) Discount allowed is debited to _________ account.

25) Drawings are deducted from ___ in the balance sheet.

26) Return inwards are deducted from_______.

27) Return outwards are deducted from _______.

28) Sacrifice ratio is calculated on _______of a partner.

29) Gain ratio is calculated on _______of a partner.

30) _______is a compulsory retirement from partnership.

31) On death of the partner amount due to him is payable to his ________.

32) Admission can take place on ______ of the financial year.

33) Admitting partner is also called as _________partner.

34) On retirement if sufficient cash balance is not available then the amount

payable to retiring partner is transferred to his ________ account.

35) On admissions of a partner he may bring goodwill in _____ form.

36) On admissions of a partner the expenses like rent are allotted in

_____ratio.

37) On admissions of a partner the expenses like advertisement are

allocated in _______ratio.

38) On admissions of a partner the expenses like loss by fire are taken on

_____basis.

39) The debtors irrecoverable are known as _______.

40) Discount allowed is allocated on the basis of _______.

Answers:-

(1- 1932 , 2 – two , 3 – credited , 4 – debited , 5 – kind, 6 – current, 7 – fluctuating, 8 – partnership deed, 9 - partnership deed , 10 – unlimited,   11 – two, 12 – 6% p.a., 13 – equal ratio, 14 - profit & loss appropriation a/c,

15 – All partners, 16 – trading a/c , 17- P & L a/c, 18 – drawings, 19 -trading result , 20 – trading a/c, 21 - P & L a/c , 22 – liability , 23- assets, 24 - P & L a/c, 25- capital , 26 – sales , 27 – purchases, 28 –admission , 29 – retirement, 30- death, 31 – legal heir, 32 – any day, 33 – incoming partner, 34 – loan a/c, 35 – cash or kind, 36 – time, 37 – sales, 38 – actual, 39 – bad debts, 40 –sales)

Topic 2 – Piecemeal Distribution of cash

❖ State whether the following statement is True or False.

1) In piecemeal distribution assets are sold out at once.	False
2) Piecemeal distribution is related to admission of the partnership.	False
3) In piecemeal distribution assets are realized and liabilities are paid out in installment.	True
4) Surplus capital method is also known as Excess Capital Method.	True
5) Under piecemeal distribution external liabilities are paid first.	True
6) Any capital balance left after all the cash distribution is over it is treated as realization loss.	True
7) Taxes paid to Government department are secured liability.	False
8) Capital balance is divided by PSR to find out unit capital	True
9) Creditors of the firm are internal liabilities.	True
10) Partner loan is external liability.	False
11) In practice assets are realized immediately after dissolution.	False
12) In piecemeal distribution General reserve are deducted from capital balance to have adjusted capital.	False
13) Amount payable to employee is treated as preferential Liability.	True
14) Realization expenses are settled first from the amount of realization.	True
15) Asset taken over by partner is debited to capital account of a partner.	True
16) Liability taken over by partner is credited to capital account of a partner.	True
17) Contingent liabilities are uncertain liabilities.	True
18) On dissolution of a firm Realization account is prepared.	True
19) Realization profit is distributed among partners in Capital ratio.	False
20) Bank overdraft is unsecured liability	True
21) Debit balance in profit & loss account is deducted from	True

capital balance to have adjusted capital.	
22) Credit balance in profit & loss account is added to capital Balance to have adjusted capital.	True

❖ **Match the following:-**

Group A	Group B
1) Bank overdraft	a) Bill under discount
2) Partners' capital balance	b) Proportionate capital method
3) Contingent liability	c) Unsecured liability
4) Excess capital method	d) Preferential liability
5) Income tax	e) Repaid at last in the process of payment
6) Partner loan	f) Internal liability

(1 – c, 2 – e, 3 – a, 4 – b , 5 – d , 6 – f)

Group A	Group B
1) Sundry creditors	a) Uncertain liability
2) Partners loan	b) Highest relative capital method
3) Contingent liability	c) Unsecured liability
4) Excess capital method	d) Preferential liability
5) Employee dues	e) Gradual realization of assets
6) Piecemeal distribution	f) Repaid before partners' capital

(1 – C , 2 – f, 3 – a, 4 – b , 5 – d , 6 – e)

❖ **Fill in the blank with correct word….**

1) Excess capital method is also known as __________.

2) The liability which depends upon happening or non-happening of the event is known as _______.

3) Under piecemeal distribution cash is realized in _________.

4) Under piecemeal distribution liabilities are settled in_______.

5) Under Excess capital method loss/profit on realization is shared by partners in ______ratio.

6) Amount due to outsider is known as ______liability.

7) Partner loan is ______liability.

8) Any amount of taxes payable to municipal authorities is considered as ________liability.

9) Payment of income tax is _______liability.

10) Adjusted capital / PSR = _________.

11) Excess capital = Adjusted capital - ___________.

12) ______ Expenses are paid first from the available cash balance before Starting the actual payment process.

13) In piecemeal distribution _______is paid at last.

14) Lowest among the unit capital is treated as _______capital.

15) General reserve is distributed among partners in ____ratio.

16) In case where at the time of distribution of cash if cash is insufficient, the Liability holders are paid ________.

17) After making payment to the external liabilities ______are paid first.

18) Partners capital is repaid at the _________in piecemeal distribution.

Answers :-

(1- Proportionate capital Method, 2-Contingent liability, 3- Parts, 4 – parts, 5- Profit sharing ratio, 6 – External liability, 7- Internal , 8- External , 9- External, 10- Unit capital, 11- Proportionate capital, 12- Realization,13 – Partners capital, 14 – Base, 15 – Profit sharing ratio, 16- Proportionately, 17 – Partners Loans,18 – last)

Topic 3. Amalgamation of the Firms

❖ State whether the following statement is True or False.

1) Amalgamation of the firm is governed by Accounting Standard 14.	True
2) In Amalgamation there is combination of two or more businesses.	True
3) Amalgamation is of the firms is done for the purpose of growth and expansion of the business.	True
4) In Amalgamation there is dissolution of old firm's takes place.	True
5) On Amalgamation old firm took over the business of new firm.	False
6) Purchase consideration is the amount payable from old firm to new firm.	False
7) Under net asset method the assets and liabilities are considered when they are taken over by new firm.	True
8) Net Asset = Liabilities taken over – Assets taken over	False
9) In realization account assets are transferred at market value.	False
10) In realization account liabilities are transferred at book value .	True
11) If any asset is taken over by partner it is debited to his account.	True
12) Liability taken over by partner is credited to his account.	True
13) The amount of purchase consideration receivable is debited to realization account.	False
14) Credit balance in realization account indicates profit on realization.	True
15) Debit balance in realization account indicates loss on realization.	True
16) Realization profit or loss is shared between the partners in capital balance ratio.	False

17) Net payment method is a method of calculating purchase consideration	True
18) At the time of P.C. calculation under Net payment method payment to creditors is not considered.	True
19) On amalgamation of the firm realization account is opened in the books of new firm.	False
20) When realization expenses are borne by new firm it is debited to realization account.	False
21) When Realization expenses are borne by old firm they are debited to realization account.	True
22) Under Purchase method for implementing the scheme of amalgamation Realization account is required to be opened.	True
23) When the amount of Purchase consideration is more than the amount of the net asset, the excess amount is treated as goodwill.	True
24) Any liability which is not taken over by partner but paid by the old firm it is credited to realization account.	False
25) Any unrecorded asset is realized is debited to bank account and credited to asset account.	True
26) If any accumulated loss are there they are distributed among partners in capital ratio.	False

Group A	Group B
1) Amalgamation	a) Current liability
2) Net asset method	b) AS – 14
3) Realization profit	c) Amalgamating firms
4) Old firms	d) Method of Purchase consideration
5) New firm	e) Shared in PSR
6) Bank overdraft	f) Amalgamated firm
7) Realization expenses	g) Debited to realization account

(1 – b , 2 – d, 3 – g, 4 – c, 5 – f, 6 – a , 7 – g)

Group A	Group B
1) General reserve	a) Method of purchase consideration
2) Realization expenses borne by new firm	b) Distributed among partners in PSR
3) Net Payment method	c) Merger of two or more firm
4) Credit balance of Realization account	d) Contingent liability
5) Debit balance of Realization account	e) Debited to Goodwill account
6) Amalgamation	f) Realization loss
7) Bill under discount	g) Realization profit

(1 – b, 2 – e , 3 – a, 4 – g, 5 – f, 6 – c , 7 – d)

❖ **Fill in the blank with correct word….**

1) Amalgamation of the firm is governed by Accounting Standard _______.

2) The objective of amalgamation of firm is to _________.

3) In amalgamation there is closure of the ______firm takes place.

4) In pure amalgamation there is dissolution of minimum ___old firms.

5) ______is the amount payable by new firm to old firm.

6) The new firm is also known as _________firm.

7) Old firms are also known as ________firms.

8) Net asset is the excess of ______over ________.

9) In the books of old firm amount receivable from new firm is credited to _____ account.

10)   Goodwill is _______ Fixed asset.

11)   Machinery is ______Fixed asset.

12)   On amalgamation the assets which are not taken over are _____.

13)   On amalgamation if there is debit balance in profit & loss account it is debited to _________ account.

14)   On amalgamation if there is balance in general reserve account it is credited to _________ account.

15)   Realization profit is shared between the partners in _____ ratio.

16)   Building & Land is ______ asset.

17)   Assets are transferred to realization account at their _____ value.

18)   Loss on realization is debited to ________ account.

19)   Payment of realization expenses are _______ to realization account.

20)   On amalgamation of the firms _______ account needs to be opened.

21)   On amalgamation of the firm there is formation of the _________.

22)   Amalgamation of firms requires minimum _______ firms.

23)   There is either _____ or ______in realization account.

24)   _______is the consideration payable by new firm to old firm.

25)   In case of amalgamation old partnership firm gets _______.

26)   If value of net assets exceeds purchase consideration there is ______ .

27)   ______is merger of two businesses.

28)   On amalgamation of firm there is ______valuation goodwill of the old firms.

Answers: -

(1- 14, 2- Increase profitability, 3 –old , 4 – two, 5- Purchase consideration,6- Amalgamated firm,7 – Amalgamating firm,8- Assets taken over liabilities taken over,9- Realization account,10- Intangible,11- tangible,12-disposed of,13- Partners capital account,14- Partners capital account, 15- Profit sharing ratio,16- tangible,17- book, 18- Partners capital account,19- debited, 20- realization,21- new firm,22- two, 23 – profit or loss, 24- Purchase consideration, 25 – dissolved, capital reserve, 27- Amalgamation, 28 - Separate)

◇◇◇◇◇◇◇◇◇◇◇◇◇◇◇◇◇◇◇◇◇◇◇◇◇◇◇◇◇◇◇◇

Topic 4. Conversion Partnership firm into Ltd. Company.

❖ State whether the following statement is True or False.

1) Conversion Partnership firm into Ltd. Company is also referred as a sale of firm to the company.	True
2) On conversion there is closure of old firm takes place.	True
3) On conversion the Ltd. company takes over the assets & liabilities of old firms.	True
4) In Company form of business liability of shareholders is unlimited.	False
5) In case of firm liability of partners is unlimited.	True
6) In case of Conversion Partnership firm into Ltd. company purchase consideration is calculated only by net asset method.	False
7) Under net asset method the market value of the asset taken over is considered.	True
8) Purchasing company has to take over all assets & liabilities of the old firm.	False
9) Old firm is also known as vendor firm.	True
10) The assets & liabilities not taken over do not form part of Purchase consideration.	True
11) When assets are taken over by the Ltd company only tangible assets are taken over.	False
12) Under net payment method the shares & debenture issued in The new company form part of the purchase consideration.	True
13) while closing the books of the old firm general reserve are Credited to partners' capital account.	True
14) While transferring the reserve to capital account they are Credited in capital ratio not in PSR.	False
15) When assets & liabilities are transferred to realization Account they are transferred at book value.	True
16) Sale of recorded asset is credited in Realization account.	True
17) Sale of un-recorded asset is not credited in Realization A/C	False
18) Unrecorded liability if paid debited to realization account.	True
19) When cash and bank balance of old firm is not taken it is not transferred to realization account.	True
20) In vertical balance sheet debentures are shown under Shareholders fund.	False

21) In vertical balance sheet debentures are shown under Long term borrowings.	True
23) In vertical balance sheet share capital & reserves are shown Under Shareholders funds.	True
24) Under trade payables creditors and bills payables are shown.	True
25) In vertical balance sheet Provisions for tax is shown under trade payables.	False
26) Securities premium is shown under reserve & surplus.	True
27) Short term investment is also termed as current investment.	True
28) Prepaid expenses are shown under short term loans & Advances in vertical balance sheet.	True
29) Bills receivables are shown under short term loans & advances in vertical balance sheet.	False
30) Debtors are shown under trade receivables in the Vertical balance sheet.	True
31) Patents are the example of tangible fixed asset.	True
32) Mining rights is an example of tangible fixed asset.	False
33) Debentures are the example of long term loans or borrowings.	True
34) In conversion no new company is formed.	False
35) In conversion there is merger of firm and limited company.	False
36) Any asset which is taken over by partner is debited to his account.	True
37) Any liability which is taken over by partner is credited to his account.	True
38) Trade mark is an intangible asset.	True
39) Long term investment are shown under current assets.	False
40) Livestock is tangible fixed asset.	True
41) Credit balance in bank account refers to bank overdraft.	True
42) Purchase consideration may be discharged by paying cash, equity shares in the new company.	True
43) Realization expenses are credited to cash account.	True

❖ **Match the following:-**

Group A	Group B
1) Land & Building	a) Amount payable by new co.
2) Copy right	b) Trade payable
3) Equity share capital	c) Prepared in the books of old firm
4) Sundry creditors	d) Tangible asset
5) Purchase consideration	e) Intangible asset
6) Realization Account	f) Part of Shareholders fund
7) Partnership business	g) Limited Liability of member
8) Company Ltd.	h) Unlimited liability of partner

(1 - d, 2 – e, 3 – f, 4 – b, 5 – a, 6 –c, 7 – h, 8 – g)

Group A	Group B
1) Plant & Machinery	a) Method of purchase consideration
2) Patents	b) Trade receivable
3) Preference share capital	c) Cash & cash equivalent
4) Sundry debtors	d) Tangible asset
5) Net Asset Method	e) Intangible asset
6) Ltd company	f) Part of Shareholders fund
7) Cash & Bank Balance	g) Shared by partners in PSR
8) Realization Profit	h) Limited liability of member

(1 - d, 2 – e , 3 – f , 4 – b , 5 – a, 6 – h , 7 – c, 8 – g)

❖ **Fill in the blank with correct word….**

1) Joint stock company form is more suitable for doing _____scale business.

2) Partnership business is has a feature of ______capital and _____liability.

3) In conversion the _____firm gets dissolved.

4) In conversion there is takeover of partnership business by _____company.

5) On dissolution realization account is opened in the books of ________.

6) ______is the brand value of the business organization.

7) In company form of business the liability of the shareholders is _____.

8) _________ the amount payable by the company ltd to the owners of old firm.

9) Assets of the firm are taken to the realization account at ________.

10) Assets & liabilities which are not taken over by the new company are

________.

11) Net asset method is a method of calculating _________.

12) Net asset = Assets taken over - ________________.

13) Under ________method no separate calculation of the P.C. is required.

14) If dissolution expenses paid by the old firm they are debited to _____.

15) Realization profit goes to the credit of _______account.

16) Realization profit/ loss is shared by partners in _____ ratio.

17) Credit balance in realization account indicates _______.

18) Debit balance in realization account indicates _______.

19) Asset taken over by partner is _______to realization account.

20) Purchase consideration receivable is recorded on the _____side of the

Realization account.

21) If dissolution expenses borne & paid by the new company it is debited to

______.

22) Old firm is also called as _______firm or ________ firm.

23) If purchase consideration exceeds the net asset value then the

   Difference is debited to ______account.

24) Trade mark is treated as _________fixed asset.

25) On conversion of firm there is _____of a new company.

26) Investment in shares & debentures are shown under _______.

27) Loose tools are parts of the _______assets of the company.

28) Cheque on hand are shown under _______in the balance sheet.

29) Balance sheet of the company is prepared as per Schedule _____ of the

   Companies Act 2013.

30) Closing stock of the Raw materials is shown under _____.

31) Overdraft from bank is shown under ________ in the balance sheet.

32) _______capital is the maximum capital of the company.

33) Authorized capital is also known as ______capital of the company.

Answers :-

(1 – Large, 2 – limited, unlimited, 3 – old, 4 – Limited, 5 – old firm,

6 – Goodwill, 7 – limited, 8 – purchase consideration, 9 – book value

10 – Disposed of, 11 – purchase consideration, 12- Liabilities taken

 over, 13- Lump sum, 14 – Realization account, 15 – Partners capital account, 16 –

Profit sharing ratio, 17 – profit , 18 – Loss, 19 – credited, 20 – Credit , 21 –

Goodwill, 22 – vendor & selling firm , 23 – Goodwill, 24 – Tangible,   25 –

Formation, 26 – Non-current investment, 27 – Current, 28 – Cash & cash

equivalent, 29 – III, 30 – Inventories, 31 – short term loans & advances,   32 –

Authorized, 33 – Nominal)

◇◇◇◇◇◇◇◇◇◇◇◇◇◇◇◇◇◇◇◇◇◇◇◇◇◇◇◇◇◇

<h1 style="text-align:center"><u>Objective questions with model answers – Sem IV</u></h1>

<u>Topic 1:- Introduction to Company accounts, Issue of shares & Debentures</u>

State whether followings statements are true or false:-

1) The company is an association of a person.	True
2) The company is an artificial person which is created by law.	True
3) The company have no perpetual succession.	False
4) The company has no separate legal status than that of its members.	False
5) The shares of the company can be easily transferred from one member to another member.	True
6) Company puts signature on the official document in form of common seal.	True
7) There are minimum 7 members required to form public company.	True
8) There are minimum 2members required to form private company	True
9) There are maximum 50 members in public company.	False
10) There are maximum 100 members in private company.	False
11) Public company can issue prospectus.	True
12) Private company can accepts deposits from general public.	False
13) If the board of company is controlled by the another company it is called as subsidiary company.	True
14) If the shares of the company is listed on the stock exchange it is called as listed company.	True
15) The auditor of government company is appointed by the directors.	False.
16) Authorized capital is mentioned in the article of association,	False.
17) The capital which is issued to the general public is called issued capital.	True
18) When the general public subscribed the part of whole of issued capital it is called as subscribed capital.	True
19) Authorized capital also called as registered capital of the company.	True
20) There are two types of shares of the company.	True

21)	Preference shareholder do not enjoy voting rights like equity share holders.	False.
22)	Equity shareholder enjoy voting rights in the company meeting.	True
23)	Equity share holders are the real risk bearers of the company.	True
24)	Equity share holders do not gets dividend if there is no Sufficient profit.	True
25)	Pref.shareholders gets dividend before equity shareholders are paid.	True
26)	Preference shareholders gets dividend at fluctuating rate of dividend.	False
27)	Equity shareholders are repaid after specific time duration.	False
28)	Preference shareholders are repaid after specific time duration.	True
29)	Preference shares can be converted into equity shares.	True
30)	In case of loss equity shareholders do not gets any dividend.	True
31)	Equity shareholders gets their capital back before preference Shareholders.	False
32)	A dividend on cumulative pref.shares accumulates every year,	True
33)	A dividend on equity shares accumulates every year,	False
34)	Sweat equity shares are issued for consideration other than cash.	True
35)	Sweat equity shares are issued to general public.	False
36)	Bonus shares are given as a gift to the existing shareholder's.	True
37)	Debentureholdres are the creditors of the company.	True
38)	Debentureholdres get return in form of interest at fixed rate.	True
39)	Debentureholdres enjoy the voting right in shareholder's meeting.	False
40)	Securities premium is part of the reserve & surplus.	True
41)	Capital reserve is non divisible profit.	True
42)	General reserve is revenue reserve.	True
43)	Capital redemption reserve is capital profit.	True
44)	Profit prior to incorporation is revenue profit.	False
45)	Secret reserve are disclosed in the balance sheet.	False
46)	Debentures are treated as short term borrowings.	False
47)	Reserve & surplus are the part of shareholders fund.	True
48)	Debentures are external source of finance.	True

49) Bills under discount is a contingent liability.	True

Match the following

Group A	Group B
1. Debentures	a) Risk capital
2. Reserve & surplus	b) Priority in dividend payment
3. Equity share capital	c) Short term liability
4. Pref. share capital	d) Nominal capital
5. Proposed dividend	e) Limited liability
6. Liability of company member	f) Minimum seven members
7. Bank overdraft	g) General reserve
8. Authorized capital	h) Current investment
9. Public company	i) Owed fund
10. Short term investment	j) Contingent liability

(1 – i , 2 – g , 3 – a, 4 – b, 5 – j, 6 - e , 7 – c, 8 – d , 9 – f , 10 – h)

Group A	Group B
1) Loan from bank	a) Last claimant
2. Reserve & surplus	b) Priority in dividend payment
3. Equity share holders	c) Short term liability
4. Pref. share capital	d) Mentioned in the MoA
5.Arrears of dividend	e) Common seal
6. Signature of company	f) Minimum two members
7. Current liability	g) Capital reserve
8. Authorized capital	h) Issued to employee
9. Private company	i) Owed fund
10. Sweat equity shares	j) Contingent liability

(1 – i , 2 – g , 3 – a, 4 – b, 5 – j, 6 - e , 7 – c, 8 – d , 9 – f , 10 – h)

Fill in the blank ------

1) Company is a ______ person created by law.

2) Liability of the member of the company is ______.

3) Minimum members required to form a public limited company is ____.

4) Minimum members required to form a private limited company is ____.

5) Maximum members in public limited company can be ____.

6) Maximum members in private limited company can be ____.

7) Management of the company is run by ______ of the company.

8) The companies registered under the special act of the government are ____companies.

9) Authorized share capital is also known as ______.

10) The companies which are listed on the stock exchanges are called ______.

11) The companies whose objective is not to earn profit are called as ______.

12) The company who control the operation of the other company is known as ____.

13) Issued capital is part of the ______share capital of the company.

14) Equity share capital is also known as ______ capital of the company.

15) Equity shareholders are known as ______ of the company.

16) ______shareholders enjoy voting right in the meeting of the company.

17) Rate of dividend on preference share capital is ______.

18) Rate of dividend on equity share capital is ______.

19) ______shares are issued free of cost to the existing shareholders of the company.

20) ______shares are issued to the employees or directors of the company without cash consideration.

21) ______ shares are convertible shares of the company.

22) Debenture is a _____ capital of the company.

23) Debenture holders are treated as _________ of the company.

24) Rate of interest on debentures is _______.

25) Debenture do not enjoy _______ in the shareholders meeting of the

company.

26) Securities premium is part of _________ in the balance sheet.

27) Owned fund is also known as _________.

28) Provision for taxation is part of _______ in the balance sheet.

29) Liquid assets are also known as ______ assets.

30) Live stock is ______ fixed assets.

31) Fixed assets = Tangible assets + __________.

32) _____ assets depreciates due to extraction.

33) Long term investment are also called as _______ investment.

34) The assets which are easily convertible into cash are called as _____.

35) Employee stock option plans are always issued for _____.

36) On buyback company has to open a special account in the bank called as

______ Account.

37) Debentures can be convertible into ______.

38) The debentures which can be transferrable by just delivery are called as ___

Debentures.

39) Secured debentures are secured against _______ of the company.

40) Debentures when issued at the amount equal to the face value they are

Called as issued at ______.

41) Debentures when issued at the amount more than its face value they are

Called as issued at ________.

42) Amount of premium received on issued is ______gain to the company.

Answers:-

(1 – Artificial, 2 – limited, 3 – Seven, 4 – two, 5 – Unlimited, 6 – 200,

7 – Directors, 8 – Statutory, 9 – Nominal capital, 10 – listed company,

11 – Nonprofit making company, 12 – Holding Company, 13 – Nominal,

14 – Risk, 15 – real owner, 16 - Equity, 17 – Fixed, 18 – Fluctuating,

19 - Bonus, 20 – Sweat equity, 21 – Preference, 22 – Loan, 23 – creditor,

24 – Fixed, 25 – voting rights, 26 – reserve & surplus, 27 – shareholders

Fund, 28 – Current liabilities, 29 – Quick, 30 – Tangible, 31 – Intangible,

32 – Wasting assets, 33 – Noncurrent, 34 – Liquid assets, 35 – Cash,

36 – Escrow, 38 – Shares, 39 – Assets, 40 – Par, 41 – Premium, 42 – Capital)

Topic 2 :- Redemption of preference shares:-

State whether followings statements are true or false:-

1) A Company can issue more than two types of capital.	False
2) Redemption of preference share capital means repayment.	True
3) Partly paid up shares cannot be redeemed.	True
4) Preference capital can be repaid out of the profits company.	True
5) CRR means Capital requirement reserve.	False
6) Preference capital can be repaid out of the proceeds of new issue of capital.	True
7) NCLT means National Company Law Tribunal.	True
8) Revaluation reserve cannot be used to W/off the premium on redemption of pref.shares.	True
9) Profit & Loss account is an example of divisible profit.	True
10) Securities premium is an example of divisible profit.	False
11) CRR refers to capital redemption reserve.	True
12) Non divisible profit can be used for redemption of pref. shares.	False
13) CRR is created out of non-divisible profit.	False
14) Revaluation reserve is an example of non-divisible profit.	True
15) Bonus shares are issued at free of cost.	True
16) Premium on redemption of shares should be adjusted out of profit.	True
17) Bank overdraft is a short term liability.	True
18) Claim of pref.shares is transferred to pref.shareholders account.	True
19) For redemption of pref.shares new shares can be issued only at par.	False
20) At time of settlement of account pref.shareholders account is Debited and cash account is credited.	True
21) Partly paid up preference shares can be redeemed.	False
22) No company can issue irredeemable preference shares.	True
23) Calls in arrears are deducted from called up capital.	True
24) Non divisible profit means the profit which cannot be utilized for Distribution of dividend.	True

Match the following:-

Group A	Group B
1) General Reserve	a) Can not be redeemed
2) Securities premium	b) Can be redeemed
3) Partly paid up shares	c) Securities premium
4) Fully paid up shares	d) Made out of divisible profit
5) Premium on redemption	e) Divisible profit
6) CRR	f) Contingent liability
7) Bills discounted	h) Non divisible profit
8) Cash & equivalent	i) Cash at bank

(1 – e , 2 – h , 3 – a , 4 – b , 5 – c , 6 – d , 7 – f , 8 – I)

Group A	Group B
1) Profit & loss account	a) Intangible asset
2) Profit prior to incorporation	b) Tangible asset
3) Goodwill	c) Long term borrowing
4) Land	d) Also Made out of divisible profit
5) Debentures	e) Divisible profit
6) Redemption of pref. shares	f) Current liability
7) Trade payables	h) Non divisible profit
8) Cash & equivalent	i) Cash at Bank

(1 – e , 2 – h , 3 – a , 4 – b , 5 – c , 6 – d , 7 – f , 8 – I)

Fill in the blanks:-

1) _______ paid up shares cannot be redeemed.

2) Redemption of capital means to __________ the share capital.

3) Premium on redemption can be adjusted from ________.

4) When redemption is carried out of profit _______ is created from divisible profit.

5) _______ Profits are available for distribution as a dividend.

6) Company can issue fresh _____ or preference shares for redemption of shares.

7) Fresh _____ cannot be issued for redemption of preference shares.

8) C.R.R means to __________.

9) Securities premium is an example of ______ profit.

10) Dividend _______ reserve is an example of divisible profit.

11) In case of nonpayment of the call Money Company may _____ shares.

12) ______ shares are issued free of cost.

13) Bill under discount is _______ liability

14) When asset is sold out ______ account is debited & ____ account is credited.

15) When asset is sold out at profit, such profit is credited to _____ account.

16) Profit on _____ of forfeited shares is transferred to capital reserve account.

17) At the time of redemption of preference shares claim is credited to

_________ account.

18) Bank overdraft is ______ liability.

19) C.R.R can be used to issue ______ shares.

20) Dividend which is not claimed by the shareholder is shown under ______.

21) Company can issue new preference shares at ____ or at ____ or at ______.

22) ______ share holder enjoy voting rights.

23) There are _____ sources for redemption of Preference shares.

24) Revaluation reserve is _____ profit.

25) Loss on sale of asset is _____ to profit & loss account.

26) Machinery is _____ asset.

27) Computer software is ______ asset.

28) Inventory is shown under _____ in the vertical balance sheet.

29) Provision for taxation is shown under _____ in vertical balance sheet.

30) Advance tax is shown under ________.

Answers:-

(1 – Partly, 2 – repay, 3 – Available profits, 4 – CRR, 5 – Divisible, 6 – Equity, 7 – Debenture, 8 – capital redemption reserve, 9 - Non divisible

10 – equalization, 11 – Forfeit, 12 – Bonus, 13 – Contingent , 14 – bank & asset, 15 – Profit & Loss, 16 – reissue , 17 – preference shareholders, 18 – Short term, 19 – Bonus, 20 – Current liability, 21 – Par,Premium,Discount, 22 – Equity shareholders, 23 – two , 24 – Non divisible, 25 – Debited , 26 – Tangible fixed, 27 – Intangible fixed, 28 – current liability, 29 – Short term provision, 30 – Short term loans and advances)

◇◇◇◇◇◇◇◇◇◇◇◇◇◇◇◇◇◇◇◇◇◇◇◇◇◇◇◇◇◇

<u>**Topic 3 :- Redemption of Debentures:-**</u>

❖ **State whether the following statement is True or False.**

1) There are two types of debentures, redeemable and irredeemable.	True
2) Redemption of debentures means paying back to the debenture holders	True
3) Discount of debentures is revenue loss to the company.	False
4) Discount on debentures can be written off from securities premium account.	True
5) Discount on issue of debenture is written off through P & L account.	True
6) Under fixed installment method the discount is written off equally over the years.	True
7) Under fluctuating installment method the amount of discount written off from P & L account goes on reducing every year.	True
8) Loss on issue of debentures is written off through P & L account	True
9) Debentures cannot be issued at par.	False
10) Debenture application money received are debited to bank account.	True
11) Debenture application money received are transferred to debentures Account.	True
12) Loss on issue of debentures are shown under current asset.	False
13) Discount on issue of debentures are shown under other non-current Asset.	True
14) Debentures are shown under shareholders fund.	False
15) There are four method of redemption of debentures.	True
16) under lump sum method repayment is made at once after certain period.	True
17) Under conversion method the debentures can be converted into equity shares.	True
18) Redemption out of profit is one of the important source of redemption.	True
19) Under redemption out of capital no profit can be utilized for redemption.	True
20) Under redemption out of capital creation of DRR account is compulsory.	False
21) Under redemption out of profit creation of DRR account is compulsory.	True
22) At the time of redemption the balance in debentures account is Transferred to debenture holder's account.	True

23) As per SEBI guidelines the total amount of redemption can be carried Out of capital.	False
24) After purchase of its own debentures company goes for cancellation of those debentures.	True
25) Debentures redemption reserve is placed under shareholders fund in the balance sheet.	False
26) After redemption balance in DRR account is transferred to capital reserve.	False
27)Debenture redemption reserve is also utilized for redemption of pref.shares.	False
28) A sinking fund is created through appropriation account.	True
29) A gain on sale of sinking fund investment is transferred to profit & Loss account.	False
30) Interest received on sinking fund investment account is credited to sinking fund account.	True
31)Balance in sinking fund account after redemption is transferred to P & L account.	False

❖ **Match the following:-**

Group A	Group B
1) CRR	a) Shareholders fund
2) DRR	b) Created for redemption of pref.shares
3) Capital reserve	c) Debentures converted into shares
4) Conversion method	d) Created for redemption of debentures
5) Balance in sinking fund a/c after redemption	e) Transferred to sinking fund account
6) Loss on sale of sinking fund investment	f) Debenture redemption fund method
7) Sinking fund method	g) Transferred to general reserve account

(1 – b, 2 – d, 3 – a, 4 – c, 5 – g , 6 – e, 7 – f)

Group A	Group B
1) Debentures	a) Cash & cash Equivalent
2) Capital reserve	b) Redemption after specified time
3) Bank balance	c) Debentures converted in shares
4) Lump sum method	d) Long term liability
5) Conversion method	e) DRR
6) Redemption out of profit	f) Reserve & surplus

(1 – d, 2 – f, 3 – a, 4 – b, 5 – c, 6 – e)

Fill in the blanks:-

1) After debentures are redeemed the balance left in sinking account is transferred to ________ account.

2) Debentures carries _____ rate of interest.

3) Debentures are shown under _____ in the balance sheet.

4) Discount on issue of debentures is _______ loss.

5) Discount on issue of debentures is shown under _______ in the balance sheet.

6) Cash in hand is shown under _____ in the balance sheet.

7) Profit on sale of sinking fund investment is transferred to _____ account.

8) General reserve is part of _____ in the balance sheet.

9) In the balance sheet sinking fund is shown under _____.

10) Under ______ method debenture holders are issued new shares.

11) Under ______ method the amount of debenture is entirely repaid on

the date of maturity.

12) Debenture is ________ capital.

13) ______ debentures creates charge on the asset of the company.

14) Under _____ method specified amount is kept aside every year out of

Profit to facilitate redemption.

15) On redemption the amount payable is transferred to ______ account.

16) In conversion debentures can be _____ or _____ converted into Shares.

17) Debenture interest paid during the year is charged to _____ account.

18) Balance in sinking fund account is transfer to ______ account.

19) Sinking fund is also known as ______ fund.

20) There is always _____ balance in sinking fund account.

Answers:-

(1 – general reserve, 2 – fixed, 3 – long term borrowing, 4 – capital, 5 –
Non-current liabilities, 6 – cash & cash equivalent, 7 – sinking fund, 8 –
Reserve & surplus, 9 – reserve & surplus, 10 – conversion, 11 – lump
Sum, 12 – Loan, 13 – Secured, 14 – sinking fund, 15 – debenture holders,
16 - Wholly or partly, 17 – Profit & loss account, 18 – general reserve,
19 – Debenture redemption fund, 20 – credit)

Topic 04 :- Profit prior to incorporation :-

❖ State whether the following statement is true or false.

1) Credit balance in trading account shows profit.	True
2) Debit balance in trading account shows loss.	True
3) Office and Admin salaries are allocated on time basis.	True
4) Carriage outward is allocated on time basis.	False
5) Discount allowed is allocated on purchase basis.	False
6) Fixed portion of the expenses are allocated on time basis.	True
7) Profit up to the date of registration is called profit prior to incorporation.	True
8) Capital profit can be used to w/off goodwill of the company.	True
9) Profit after the date of registration is called post incorporation profit.	True
10) Prior period profit is treated as goodwill.	False
11) Dividend on shares is post incorporation expenses.	True
12) Director salary is pre incorporation expenses.	False
13) Postage expenses is allocated on time basis.	True
14) Vendors salary are charged to pre incorporation period.	True
15) Management expenses are allocated on sales basis.	False
16) Irrecoverable debts are allocated on sale basis.	True
17) Sales promotion expenses are allocated on sale basis.	True
18) Interest payable on purchase consideration is to be shared in time basis.	True
19) Fees payable to the director to be allocated to pre incorporation period.	False
20) Turnover ratio is also called as sales ratio.	True
21) Time ratio is decided on the basis of no. of months in pre and post incorporation period.	True
22) Sales ratio is decided on the basis of value of sales in pre and post incorporation period.	True
23) Depreciation on delivery vehicle is to be allocated on time basis.	False

❖ Match the following:-

Group A	Group B
1) Pre Incorporation profit	a) Sales ratio
2) Post Incorporation profit	b) Goodwill
3) Fixed expenses	c) Charged to Pre Incorporation period
4) Free samples	d) Charged to Post Incorporation period
5) Vendor salary	e) Time ratio
6) Shares transfer fees	f) Profit & loss account
7) Pre Incorporation Loss	g) Capital reserve

(1 – g , 2 – f , 3 – e , 4 – a , 5 – c , 6 – d , 7 – b)

Group A	Group B
1) Salary of office staff	a) Who sells the business
2) Advertisement	b) Who starts the new business
3) Partners salary	c) Post incorporation expenses
4) Share transfer fees	d) Pre incorporation expenses
5) Promoter	e) Turnover ratio
6) Vendor	f) Time ratio

(1 - f , 2 – e , 3 – d, 4 – c , 5 – b , 6 – a)

Fill in the blanks:-

1) Pre incorporation stage is also known as ______ stage.

2) Profit earned before ________ is transferred to capital reserve account.

3) Post earned after the date of registration is transferred to ____ account.

4) Time ratio is calculated on the basis of ____ period & ____ period.

5) Sales ratio is calculated on the basis of ____ during the pre incorporation period and post incorporation period.

6) Sales ratio is also known as ______ ratio.

7) If the date of takeover is 1st April 2021 and date of Incorporation is 1st August 2021 and year ending is 31st March 2022,then the time ratio is ________.

8) If the date of takeover is 1st January 2021 and date of Incorporation is 1st August 2021 and year ending is 31st Dec 2022 ,then the time ratio is _________.

9) If sales during the pre incorporation period is Rs 200,000 and post incorporation period is Rs.5,00,000 then the sales ratio is ______.

10) If sales during the pre incorporation period is Rs 300,000 and post incorporation period is Rs.6,00,000 then the sales ratio is ______.

11) If the sales during the year is Rs.12,00,000 and pre Incorporation sales is Rs. 3,00,000 then the sales ratio is _______.

12) The fixed expenses are allocated on _______ ratio.

13) Printing & stationery expenses are allocated in ____ ratio.

14) General expenses are allocated on ____ ratio.

Answers:-

(1 – pre registration stage, 2 – Incorporation, 3 – Profit & loss a/c, 4 – pre incorporation period & post incorporation period, 5 – sales made, 6 – Turnover ratio, 7 – 1:2 , 8 – 7:5 , 9 – 2:5 , 10 – 1:2 , 11 – 1:3 , 12 – Time ratio , 13 – Time ratio , 14 – Time ratio)

◇◇◇◇◇◇◇◇◇◇ **LAST PAGE**◇◇◇◇◇◇◇◇◇◇◇◇